Summary of The 7 Habits of Highly Effective People

Powerful Lessons in Personal Change by Stephen R. Covey

Summareads Media

Get 2 summary books that we're giving away for FREE. Visit:

www.summareads.com

Table of Contents

INTRODUCTION - Notes from SummaReads Media Team

Almost a countless number of self-help books are written every year. Very few become best sellers and even fewer survive the test of time. Covey's 7 Habits of Highly Effective People has flourished since 1989. Millions have adopted this timeless approach to a fulfilling life. Every day, new readers discover his book through word-of-mouth as well as professional recommendations. Covey reveals the tools necessary for finding enduring self-happiness as well as for nurturing effective interpersonal relationships in marriages, parenting, businesses, organizations, and other social encounters.

Businesses, big and small, have also changed cultures and increased success by implementing the *7 Habits of Highly Effective People*. Recognizable names include FedEx, McDonalds of Brazil, Hertz Car Rentals, and Fred Meyer Stores just to name a few. Each has a different story of what they achieved. For Fred Meyer it was increasing employee loyalty. McDonalds wanted a culture where employees wanted to work. FedEx sought out better technology implementation. Hertz achieved continuous improvement with a more effective management team.

The book progresses through the seven sequential steps needed to first transform yourself and then expand your self-understanding and self-values into every aspect of your life. The result is a synergy that you are able to share with everyone.

POWER PRINCIPLES

- **Part One** of the book brings into the spotlight that any and all changes you want in your life must begin with you. History is full of examples for you to follow but your true meaning and happiness in life flows from ingraining "character ethics" at the core of everything you do.

- **Part Two** is the beginning of the first three habits. This is where you begin changing yourself before you can change how you interact with others. This is where you get your own house in order. Becoming highly effective requires that you have a clear vision of what you will accomplish in life.

- **Habit 1** begins part two of the book by jumping right into you becoming the leader and manager of your own life. You alone have the ability to change the circumstances of your life. Your future is only limited by the actions you begin taking today.

- **Habit 2** is the first of the two necessary steps needed to transform yourself as a person to lead the life envisioned for yourself and those you interact with. It is the descriptive vision of your life to come.

- **Habit 3** is the second necessary step for change by providing the tools you need to make real change happen. Key among these is your ability to manage your time and actions. By differentiating between what seems urgent in your life and what is truly important, you become able to affect meaningful change.

- The cumulative effect of the first three habits is you maturing from a person dependent on others to being fully independent.

- **Part Three** of the book moves the focus from your self-growth to interacting with all others who you encounter in life. Key to this is understanding your circle of influence and how to grow it.

- **Habit 4** defines how your interdependence with others evolves into powerful outcomes when you relinquish unsatisfying consequences in favor or win-win solutions. The goal becomes combining your self-confidence with empathy for others. Both you and those that you engage with become fully committed to success when you share the same goals.

- **Habit 5** provides a remarkable ability to influence people in a way they want to be influenced. It involves deeply understanding the perspective of others so that your interactions have the most direct meaning to them as possible. Habit 5 develops the missing but key communication tool of empathic listening.

- **Habit 6** brings the other habits to bare as fully on your life as possible. It's really quite simple. Once you have your own life in order and are working effectively with others, synergy flows throughout all of your activities. The sum of the whole is much more satisfying and powerful than the individual pieces. The result of bringing it all together is the purposeful life that all of us seek.

- **Part Four** of the book brings everything full circle once you have achieved the basics. Life is a process of constantly maturing. You will have the tools needed to grow and age into the person you have always wanted to be.

- **Habit 7** is no more than finding the time and devotion needed to renew ourselves physically, spiritually, mentally, and socially. After you overcome procrastination, you need to maintain the momentum using the same tools that you have mastered. The rest of your life is now fully under your control.

SUPER

SUMMARY

Part One: YOUR VISION OF THE BEST YOU CAN BE

Covey does not create his view of living a life of enduring happiness out of whole cloth. In the opening and throughout the book, he cites philosophers, writers, thinkers, and doers who have graced mankind throughout history. Covey shares insights and inspiration of what it means to live a remarkable life of notable accomplishments.

Before unraveling the secrets in the book, he questioned his own balance of personal and work life – "I don't know my wife and children anymore." His own self-value was also questioned as he came to understand that in spite of taking several time-management courses, he struggled to keep up with everything that needed to be done every waking hour of every day.

It's during this stage of his life that Covey questions if his life brings any real consequences for others or himself - regardless of all his efforts. One reality that he did understand is that his life almost completely lacked the happiness, peace, and fulfillment that would bring contentment.

It's not that he felt he had no control over his life and the outcomes. Covey believed that he could find solutions to problems, get along well with others, and achieve goals. But still, he felt that his personality was contrived. That much of his achievement came from manipulating others to control the outcome.

Covey comes to believe it is this contrived way of life that will always fall short of achieving fulfillment, satisfaction, and ultimately happiness. It is through observation of his own contrived life that the enlightened solution became a Principle Based Life.

The result was, he decided to research self-fulfilling prophecies or the "Pygmalion Effect." What he discovered is that our lives are the embodiment of our perceptions. That by examining and changing our perceptions when necessary, our lives become "successful" by our own definition.

Hence, we must examine our perceptions as the root of how we find self-success.

Give Your Perceptions a Noble Cause

Importantly, awareness of these self-fulfilling prophecies and that our own perceptions are at the root of our happiness is the only key needed to enable self-defined success in life. It begins by validating our perceptions and refining these if necessary (which is usually the case). Next, we must strive to make our actions support our perceptions. Ultimately, our actions control our life experiences and our experiences define our success.

You might find this all to be self-evident. That we control our own destiny and that we are most likely to achieve the destiny that we define by our perceptions. Covey concluded that you would be right.

What enabled Covey to unravel the mystery of the 7 Habits also involved his study of contemporary writings on self-help and self-improvement. What he found is that people had become fixated on superficial appearances and short-term goals. A "keeping up with the Jones" mentality. Contemporary man has become fixated on self-help and self-improvement that is self-serving.

In contrast, Covey found that historically enduring literature, philosophies, and views of life were not self-serving. Rather, what stood the test of time were perceptions and actions that improved the long-term human experience as a whole rather than the short-term pleasure of the individual.

Covey calls this the "**Character Ethic**."

He calls the contemporary fixation on superficial appearances the "Personality Ethic."

At the true root of *7 Habits of Highly Effective People* is the need to shift perceptions (and actions) away from the Personality Ethic towards the Character Ethic. Personality being the outside that you present to the world and your character being responsible for your inner happiness.

But it's not as simple as just making your inner-self happy. A bad ethic and bad actions bring you many more troubles than satisfaction. Stealing money from your employer may give you the money to buy happiness but spending five years in jail will not!

What character ethics is about is the long-term satisfaction that comes from "integrity, humility, fidelity, temperance, courage, justice, patience, industry, simplicity, modesty, and the Golden Rule." These are the long enduring ethics that Covey found in historically enduring writings. For example, the Preamble to U.S. Constitution promotes what is good for the many with the phrase, "insure domestic tranquility, provide for the common defense, promote the general welfare, and secure the blessings of liberty to ourselves and our posterity." This is about the many rather than the self, which is also similar to the autobiography of Benjamin Franklin.

That is not to say the Covey discards the personality ethic entirely. Certainly, there is value in what is being taught today in the way of skills, effective communication techniques, positive thinking, and even methods of influencing others. But these are secondary traits that are most useful when these enhance the more basic character ethic.

Covey provides several examples of when personality ethic supersedes character ethic, the result is a lack wholesomeness and endurance of the person. Notably, he points out how some people rise to social prominence through personality ethics such as greed and manipulation but have little or no long-lasting influence when these are not built on a foundation of character ethics.

We may even work with people who are able to enthusiastically communicate what we want to hear. But their actions are more powerful than words. If their underlying actions fail to support us individually or the good of the many, we soon become disillusioned and no longer follow them or hold them up as an inspirational example. Character ethics are the foundation that personality ethics can only build higher upon.

The Character Ethic is a Paradigm Shift

Your perceptions create the paradigm that you follow. Covey uses several examples to explain this. One example is a mislabeled map. He explains that if you are given a map of Detroit but it is labeled as Chicago, you can become convinced that you will find where you want to go although your map is fundamentally wrong.

Another analogy is that if the perception of your environment is that you can't trust anyone, nor any institution, nor any belief system, that you will never find where you want to go. Your perception creates your map and your map is the paradigm that you live in.

Your paradigm affects how you act. You portray attitudes and behaviors that support your paradigm – your map. When your paradigm lacks integrity, so will your attitude and behavior. If your paradigm is that most people are out to get you, you will not behave in a way that is helpful to others. You will be suspicious of everyone and everything. You will miss out on many opportunities that otherwise would have good consequences for yourself and others.

This is why you must shift your paradigm. Only when your map has integrity, can you recognize ideas and actions that have integrity.

How important is a **paradigm shift**? The United States Constitution was a paradigm shift. The founders looked around at the same world as King George viewed but the founders saw a different paradigm. King George's self-serving paradigm was forced to relinquish the paradigm that served the people. That new paradigm has stood the test of time to become the model for many other societies of the world.

How many times have great scientific discoveries come from paradigm shifts? Major paradigm shifts include the fact that our earth revolves around the sun and that disease is caused by forces much smaller than humans in the form of one-celled bacteria. Paradigm shifts create a completely new way of viewing the world. Paradigm shifts create powerful changes in our world and in us as individuals.

You can spend a lifetime working on personality ethics to briefly improve how those around see you as a person. Even if you lack character ethics, you will likely enjoy some temporary admiration from others. What you are really doing is working to change how others perceive you. You are doing very little work to change the person you are on the inside. Maybe that is all you are looking for in your definition of a successful and happy life. But if you believe a major change is needed, look to a paradigm shift based on developing character ethics.

Paradigm Shifts are Seldom Instant

You've probably had an epiphany that changes how you view something. An epiphany often occurs instantly during an everyday situation. Instantly, it changes how you view that particular and similar situations. But it doesn't change your perception of the entire world or your place in life. A paradigm shift is much more powerful because it changes everything about how you view and interact with the world.

This is what is necessary to transform from a personality-based ethic to a character-based ethic. You must stop looking for how the world affects you and shift towards how you want to affect the world. The world does not revolve around you. Whatever the world does to impact you will be a very small impact compared to the impact you can have on the world.

Just to begin a paradigm shift, you must first suspend your current perceptions. This begins by examining what **principles** will define who you want to be. This includes suspending a belief in a set of principles belonging to a specific faith or religion. At the least, empowering a full paradigm shift requires fully examining the principles of every long-lasting religion, social philosophy, and ethical system. From these, you look for the principles that are self-evident. These are principles that do not need a long list of logical arguments to arrive at the conclusion. Self-evident principles apply in every circumstance. You don't pick and choose between multiple self-evident principles to decide which one applies to a certain circumstance. These will not conflict with each other.

You might think of self-evident principles as the rules applying to society in the way that the laws of nature apply to the world as whole. You cannot find a reason to change self-evident principles.

Returning to the founding fathers of the US Constitution, they eloquently expressed the value of self-evident principles as, ""We hold these truths to be self-evident: that all men are created equal and endowed by their Creator with certain inalienable rights, that among these are life, liberty, and the pursuit of happiness."

There are many principles for consideration. Among these are honesty, integrity, a sense of service to make a contribution, and respect for human dignity. There are many self-evident principles that are not followed by most people; "time is more valuable than money" and "to give more than you take." One suggestion from Covey to test principles is:

> *"One way to quickly grasp the self-evident nature of principles is to simply consider the absurdity of attempting to live an effective life based on their opposites. I doubt that anyone would seriously consider unfairness, deceit, baseness, uselessness, mediocrity, or degeneration to be a solid*

*foundation for lasting happiness and success." - Stephen
Covey*

If you have not been living a life based on principles or a
character ethic, all is certainly not lost. Life is a series of
steps and growth. Many, if not most people, live their entire
life without purposefully examining other paradigms. These
are people who are looking for shortcuts that brought about
a society based on personality ethics. A paradigm based on
principles that value outward appearances and acceptance
more than the development of character.

Covey shares several examples. One is displaying an attitude
and behavior to others that you are an accomplished concert
hall piano player when reality is that you only have beginner
skills. You'll be found out and the result will be
embarrassment and losing the trust of those you once had
convinced. A life based on character ethics acknowledges
beginner skills with an attitude for becoming concert
quality. Rather than suffering humiliation and loss of trust,
you take the needed development actions and receive
encouragement and help from those wanting to see you
succeed.

In the business world, executives try to achieve change or
growth in many ways that require very little value-added
effort on their own part. They give speeches, enforce tough
rules on employees, or merge with a more successful
competitor. When one or more fails, they continue trying
other suggestions found in multiple self-help business

books. All without trying the most time tested of all, which is demonstrating integrity and honesty to develop a high-trust organization where everyone benefits.

Understanding the Underlying Problem

A paradigm shift may be exactly what you need if you have trouble understanding what the underlying problem really is. Leaders, bosses, and individuals make changes with the honorable intent of improving an organization or relationship. Often, the honorable attempt at change is a stern lecture explaining how good the people have it in their current situation. Or more training to demonstrate better ways of doing things. In dramatic situations, people are fired and relationships end. All without considering that it could be the boss' own behavior that is holding back the organization or relationship from improving.

Do those you are interacting with believe you are acting in their best interest? The underlying problem very well could be you rather than them. If you are finding strong evidence of a personality ethic in yourself, this is where you want to begin looking at what the true problem is and what it will take to solve it.

The problem may not even be in the way you treat others. Maybe you are trying to live by a principle that you are conflicted about. Your organization or relationship could be working at top performance with no room for meaningful improvement. It could be that you are conflicted about how to best use the time, money, and resources available.

Understanding this about yourself could bring on the realization that the real problem and real solution will come from a paradigm shift within you without outside action from others.

The important lesson here is that you cannot solve significant problems by continuing to think in the same manner as caused the problem in the first place. – paraphrased from Albert Einstein

Only you can decide if the underlying problem requires a paradigm shift as radical as moving from a personality ethic to a character ethic. But if you are ready for a principle-centered and character-based solution, it begins by adopting the 7 Habits. This is also a way towards continued self-renewal as you first understand who you are, who you want to become, and what you can become after that.

None of This Will Be Easy

One of the reasons people have been pulled into the personality ethic is because it is easier than the character ethic. The personality ethic is gratifying to us as individuals without considering if it is satisfying to others. Even more self-serving is that results are often instantly gratifying. These are not easy rewards to give up today with an uncertain hope that the rewards of tomorrow will be even more gratifying.

There is **risk**. A paradigm shift will change how you experience the entire world. It takes a brave person to give up what is familiar to venture into the unknown. But take encouragement from the many who have gone before you. Our democratic government required an entirely new foundation without a blueprint. Immigrants by the millions have left homelands in search of a better life. On the American continents, mankind has continued to pioneer the west and the north. When no new frontiers seemed to exist, man left the earth for the moon and then stretched far out into space. By journeying over new horizons, mankind improves who he is and redefines what is possible.

What you explore here are only new habits. You are learning a new way to govern yourself - not traveling to the stars. Still, habits can be hard to change, especially habits of a lifetime. Covey explains three components that go into a habit.

1. The knowledge that you want to do something and the knowledge of what it is you want to do. This is the new paradigm that you need to create.

2. The skills needed to achieve the new habit. With a new paradigm, you'll need to learn and practice new skills.

3. The motivation to follow through with the new habit. For many, this requires unlearning or ignoring what your old habits taught you to want and expect. Stopping old habits is just as difficult as starting new habits.

Covey defines happiness this way, "in part at least, as the fruit of the desire and ability to sacrifice what we want now for what we want eventually." He also sees this as progress along a continuum that is as natural as maturing as a person. This makes progress both difficult and easier at the same time. It's easier because we have plenty of experience with growth towards maturity. We have all experienced infancy, childhood, puberty, teenage years, and young adulthood. Most of us were nurtured by parents and role models through these phases until we became adults and were considered mature. Some people may have difficulty continuing to mature in adulthood without being nurtured by others.

Paradigm shifts require self-nurturing. You are no longer dependent on others to tell you what to think and how to act. You become an independent person responsible for your own happiness, success, and independent thinking. You are responsible for everything that defines who you are as a person.

At the same time, your paradigm must embrace how you interact with all of the people that you have relationships with. This includes people still living the paradigm of the personality ethic. The personality ethic is so deeply entrenched in our society that trying to change others is futile. Your paradigm must include how to effectively work with all others, how to effectively communicate with people outside of your paradigm, how to be a good team member, and all other things that go into interpersonal relationships. Be aware that the personality ethic places individuals on their own pedestal, but a character ethic places principles on your pedestal. In the most difficult situations, you may conclude that you need to change your circumstances and that could well be the right thing to do. But a change in circumstances will not change who you are unless you change your paradigm.

This new paradigm may be difficult to adjust to and achieve at first. It requires you to think and act independently while simultaneously striving to maximize your effectiveness by relating to people you are interdependent with. Independence and interdependence can seem contradictory. What you need to understand is that even when working at your best, you will achieve much more by working with others. If you have ever wondered where the phrase "win-win" came from, it is the 4th of Covey's 7 habits. "Synergy" is another phrase closely associated with these principles.

Two Parts to Effectiveness

Becoming highly effective requires that you master being both independent and interdependent. The sequence to achieving this is to first become independent. That is the purpose of Habits 1, 2, and 3.

The 7 Habits are presented sequentially so that each build upon the previous. The first three habits are together in Part Two: Become the Person You Want to Be. These are the habits needed for the paradigm shift from personality ethic to character ethic. These are also the habits for moving from being dependent on others to becoming an independent person. You cannot engage in highly effective interdependent relationships until you are first independent. Equally important is that people dependent on others can never have interdependent relationships. There is no shortcut to becoming highly effective without embracing habits 1 through 3.

Habits 4, 5, and 6 come in Part Three: Playing and Working Well with Others. This is how others begin to perceive who you are. It is about developing trust that evolves into effective teamwork, cooperation, and effective communication. By becoming interdependent with others, you are able to leverage synergy into your life. This is where the most power from the 7 Habits comes from. You will be able to make independent choices and decisions while at the same time working effectively with others to achieve what you cannot achieve alone. Choose carefully where you put your effort here because the rewards for everyone involved need to be progressing towards happiness and success. Individuals do not need to be seeking the same rewards or goals. However, the contributions of each individual needs to contribute to the rewards of all others.

It's not necessary to master Habits 1, 2, and 3 before moving to Habits 4, 5, and 6. But it is important to understand that a sequence is involved. The more proficient you become at the first three determines how successful you will be with Habits 4, 5, and 6.

Habit 7 stands alone in Part Four: Completing the Circle Again and Again. This reinforces that you don't have to first master Habits 1-3 nor Habits 4-6. Habit 7 is the **continuum**

of progress and growth. Another way of thinking about it is as continuing to mature. Habit 7 should be the easiest of the habits because it circles around for more self-improvement via the other six habits. There will be substantial room for growth but the territory will be familiar. You will already have gone through the basic paradigm shift.

The habits and synergy that results are the foundation for increasing your effectiveness. Covey uses the analogy of the goose that lays the golden egg. At the heart of the analogy is that there is no shortcut to obtaining what you want out of life. In the story, the farmer butchers the goose to harvest all of the golden eggs at once. Of course, there are no more golden eggs. The golden eggs only come through the process that produces eggs. The *7 Habits of Highly Effective People* is the process you need if you want many golden eggs.

The 7 Habits begin with inward examination and improvement.

Part Two: BECOME THE PERSON YOU WANT TO BE

This is about moving from dependence to independence. But first, you must realize you are already unique just by being human. A key characteristic separating human from other animals is our unique ability to think. Specifically, to think about our own thinking process. We have the ability to "think in mathematical terms" or "think in religious terms" or "think in terms of principles."

We begin by thinking in "terms of being proactive." With self-awareness and the realization that we can change ourselves. We can change how we think.

Chapter 1: Assuming Leadership of Your Own Life (Be Proactive)

How we 'see' things or how we 'think' is "the most fundamental paradigm of effectiveness." This is at the root of everything about us from our attitude to the actions we take. How we think is the map that we follow through life. To go somewhere else in life, we must first change how we think.

In the personality ethic, we think almost exclusively about how others see and perceive us. We almost never think about "who we are" or about "our inner-self." Yet, this is the most basic characteristic separating us from other animals. To grow as humans, we need to take control and grow who we are as individuals.

It has become common in today's society to blame who we have become on our environment – "we are a product of our environment." Doing this completely ignores your ability and responsibility to be the person that you want to be. Instead of being a product of your environment, you have the exclusive ability to change your environment. You could say that who you are is a result of your DNA or your upbringing. Yet our world is full of people who had a tough start in life and found a way to achieve greatness. They did it by making an independent choice that was not dependent on their environment. You too have the ability to make that choice.

With self-awareness comes imagination. The ability to imagine different circumstances for yourself and for others. Without imagination, you cannot create a different map that will lead you to where you want to go in life. Neither animals nor computers have imagination. Our human imagination enables self-determination.

Becoming "**proactive**" (habit 1) is about more than just taking action. It's about being accountable and responsible for that action. Blaming your life on circumstances and environment is ignoring responsibility for your life. Accepting your circumstances is reactive. Changing your circumstances is proactive. Your circumstances include everything involved in your life. It includes your financial circumstances, your educational achievements, your social position, your career, and everything about how you define yourself. It includes the principles and values that you choose to live with or without.

This doesn't mean that you ignore your circumstances or environment. That is your reality right now. The choice you have is whether to stay in those circumstances and simply to react to what happens or to become proactive to change your circumstances and what happens. Covey uses several quotes from people who obtained greatness from humble beginnings to illustrate this ability to make self-determining choices. One is Gandhi's, "They cannot take away our self-respect if we do not give it to them."

Everyone does not start from the same beginning. Some people reach self-determination with a few short steps because they began from circumstances that include an advanced education and many opportunities in life. Others are much less fortunate because they have experienced a lifetime of difficulties without opportunities. Admittedly, people from difficult circumstances have a much longer path to follow but they still have the choice to begin traveling that path. For them, achieving happiness and success may be a smaller portion compared to what the more advantaged have the opportunity to achieve. But the disadvantaged can make achievements beyond their current circumstances and through interdependence and interaction (including future generations) improve future circumstances.

For a real life example, Covey combines Gandhi's perception of self-respect with a nurse's experience of caring for a wretched old man that showed no respect and had no appreciation for anything she did for him. By examining her inner-awareness, the nurse became aware that the old man was making her entire life miserable because she allowed him to take away her self-respect. By regaining her self-respect, she was able to disregard the misery the cantankerous old man was attempting to inflict on her. It was her choice, not his, if she would wallow in miserable circumstances.

> *"We have all known individuals in very difficult circumstances, perhaps with a terminal illness or a severe physical handicap, who maintain magnificent emotional strength. How inspired we are by their integrity! Nothing has*

a greater, longer lasting impression upon another person than the awareness that someone has transcended suffering, has transcended circumstance, and is embodying and expressing a value that inspires and ennobles and lifts life."

\- Stephen Covey

Your attitude paradigm has the power to inspire yourself and others or to pull everyone down into misery.

Find Solutions

Being proactive is about taking initiative. Don't confuse it with being overly aggressive or demanding. You'll never effectively interact with others through bullying. People interact and become interdependent when you offer solutions. If solutions were simple, they would occur to everyone. But solutions don't simply pop up out of thin air. Finding solutions requires initiative.

If you want a better or different job, it takes initiative. At the least, you'll need to determine what that job is. Then you'll need to find where the job is available and apply for it. But more likely, it will take more initiative than that. After you decide what job you want, you may need to acquire the skills needed. That may require more education or an apprenticeship for a low amount of pay. For an executive position, it may require first studying the problems a particular industry needs solutions to. And then presenting a solution to the problems as part of the interview process.

Right about now, you may be thinking this is all about positive thinking. Yes, your attitude is about positive thinking and that might keep you in a good mood but it won't change your circumstances. To change your circumstances you must have an attitude that everything can be better and then take the initiative to make it better. The two combined are proactive.

A good place to begin becoming more proactive is by becoming more aware of the **language** you use and change it if needed. A reactive person speaks and thinks with words that accept the circumstances. They use blame words such as blaming it on DNA or being a victim of their own emotions. Proactive words express the current situation and speak about alternatives that can change it. Proactive thinking and talking also weighs the consequences of not taking action and the possible outcomes of different alternatives. Weighing the consequences before taking action leads to better decision making.

Understand Your Circle of Influence

This is how you use your time, energy, and resources effectively. What you are concerned about and what you can actually influence are not always the same. You can be concerned that a terrible flood is coming your way but you have no influence to stop it. Your influence lies within your ability to work with your community to survive and minimize damage the flood might cause.

It's only within your circle of influence that being proactive is effective. Of course, this comes back to making decisions. When faced with a concern or circumstance that you want to change, you must first consider what you can influence. This includes deciding between different alternatives that you have. Your circle of influence increases as your interdependence with others increases. Facing a flood, you could choose only trying to save your family and belongings. You may even be successful. But without the synergy of the community, the schools your children attend and the grocery store you shop at might not survive. Through **interdependence** you expand your circle of influence.

By being proactive, you change your circumstances. This changes your position, wealth, role, and relationships. As your circumstances change, your circle of influence becomes larger. Through continuous growth (Habit 7), your circle of influence may one day become larger than your circle of concern. Part of your responsibility as a highly effective person means effectively prioritizing and applying your larger circle of influence. Continuous growth may include expanding your circle of concern when your circle of influence achieves the ability to make greater changes.

There are degrees to your circle of influence. Outside the circle of influence are concerns you have no control over. Inside your circle of influence is what you have either direct or in-direct control over. This brings us back to the first six habits. Through Habits 1-3, you have direct control over your inner-self. With Habits 4-6, you have in-direct control through interdependence with others.

Returning to the language of speaking and thinking, your language helps define your circle of influence. These are words like "have" and "be." If you must "have" something to change your circumstances, it is outside your direct circle of influence. When you can change circumstances by "being" different, it is inside your direct circle of influence. If your "concern" is paying off the mortgage on your home, you need to "have" more money that you can't directly influence. If you can "be" more budget conscious, it is in your direct circle of influence. Pay attention to what you think you need to "have" compared to what you can "be." Being proactive is about being more resourceful, being more loving, being organized, etc. Habit 1 begins with being proactive where you have the most influence.

Becoming proactive does take a paradigm shift for many people. It requires no longer placing the blame for your circumstances on others. It requires being proactive to use your influence to change your circumstances.

Being proactive has consequences that involve your principles. You can change your circumstances by being dishonest by robbing a bank or your boss. But if you are caught, your circumstances will reflect the principles you used to make the decision.

Commitment and promises also have an important role in how effective we become. For the inner-self, it becomes a matter of honor to follow through on commitments and keep promises. By keeping our commitments, we build integrity both within ourselves and with others. We grow our strength to take on bigger responsibilities. We increase our circle of influence and our effectiveness.

Chapter 2: Determining the Life You Choose to Lead (Begin With the End)

Covey begins explaining Habit 2 by having you envision your own funeral. Take notice of who attends and what they say about you and your character. What did they admire, what did they learn from you, and what will you be remembered for? What is your legacy? Did you make a difference for having lived?

Envisioning your own funeral puts you in touch with your fundamental values. These are what you find important about living your life. These define your happiness and success. At the core of this lesson is what you need to be doing today with **the end in mind**. What behaviors and actions can you take today, tomorrow, next month, and into the future to be the person you want to be.

At the very least, you want to be sure today's behaviors and actions do not go against the **values** you have identified as being important to you. Take neutral actions if you have to. You might not be able to immediately align all of your actions with where you want to go, but you can begin creating your map of how to get there.

Most of us are so busy with daily activities that we never step back to see where our actions are taking us. Covey's analogy is climbing a corporate ladder only to reach the view from the top and realizing you climbed the wrong ladder. This happens to people from all walks of life. Plumbers become plumbers because that is what their father did. Daughters become doctors because that is what mother wanted them to become. No matter how hard you work, if you're going down the wrong path you will arrive at the wrong place.

If you want a life of fulfillment, you need to at least understand what you determine to be success. Covey says, "all things are created twice." That we must first create a **mental picture** of them before we can create them in our **reality**. Almost everything we do in life begins with a plan. If you are going to take a trip, you plan the route on a map or call the airline for a schedule. If you are building a house, you start with plans. If you are starting a business, you decide what to sell and how you will sell it. Even our daily activities such as grocery shopping begin with a list of what we plan to buy. Taking responsibility for your life means having a life-fulfilling plan.

As you enact the plan, you begin with your circle of influence and as that grows; you are able to move closer to what you envision. If we don't plan our lives, we live a life of default. We live a life according to the circumstances given to us. We complain that we would work harder if we had a better boss. We complain that life would be much better if we had a better education. We complain that we would be healthier if our wife stocked healthier food in the refrigerator. Everything becomes a default because we don't have a plan to change our circumstances… and so life goes on in default mode.

We remain dependent on others. Independence requires that you have a plan for your life and that you take action to make it your reality.

> *"Habit 1 says, You are the creator. Habit 2 is the first creation."* – Stephen Covey

Habits 1 and 2 are about leadership and management. Leadership and management are not the same. Leadership is about creating a vision. In habit 1, leadership is about you becoming independent to control who you are and who you will become. In Habit 1, leadership is the first part of "all things are created twice." As the leader of your life, you create the plan for the rest of your life. Leadership is the ability to do the right thing.

In habit 2, management is the ability to do it right. In "all things are created twice," management is the second creation that turns the right vision into your reality.

Don't underestimate the value of your leadership role. Leadership is how you know you are following the right map in life. Management navigates the curves in the road and makes sure the car is kept in good operating condition. Being effective requires both. But keep in mind that **leadership comes before management**. Make sure you have the right map before beginning to navigate your trip. There may be times when you want to change where you are going in life. This is a time to resume the leadership role to either change the map or decide to take a different route on the same map. Then you can again resume managing the navigation on the different map or new route.

In interdependent relationships, you have to know what role you are in at the time. There will be times when you assume the leadership to point out the best direction to take. There will also be times when leadership is shared so that synergy determines the best path to take. This is often the case in marriages and other close relationships. There are also times when you allow others to assume the leadership role and you manage what is happening to make sure it is done correctly. As an independent person, you are always responsible for both roles to determine what you want to accomplish and how to accomplish it.

The paradigm shift needed in Habit 2 is changing your life into something different from what others have already created for you. Habit 2 requires that through self-awareness we examine the path we are following in life. That we self-determine if we are adhering to values and principles that have been given to us as a default path to follow. A path defined by someone or some circumstance that is not aligned with what we most value. When you discover it is not the path you want, you must use your power of imagination to redraw the map based on your values and principles.

To begin with the end in mind, means beginning with clear values, principles, and direction. It means creating a paradigm where behaviors and actions are in agreement with those values and direction. It means creating a habit of making decisions based on values and principles. When facing the most challenging decisions is when these values and principles are most needed as a map. This is the character ethic that you can live with rather than the personality ethic that puts up a false face to others of what is most important to you.

Your Mission in Life

Covey recommends creating a personal "mission statement" as a first step to "begin with the end in mind." It should define what you intend to contribute or accomplish with your life based on your values and principles. It will be highly unique to you. One format it could resemble is the Constitution of the United States. It should be able to endure throughout time with little or no change. Your mission statement should be strong enough to take you through conflicts as divisive as the Civil War. It should be what every decision you make can be evaluated against. It should be the inspiration that directs your path in life.

The world around you will change constantly. People become frustrated, disillusioned, and burned out when they are constantly trying to change their values and principles to align with the changing world around them. This demonstrates the importance of including "self-evident" values and principles in your mission statement. Self-evident values never change. These become your bedrock in an ever-changing world. From this unshakable foundation, you build your short- and long-term goals, from which your "proactive" life emerges (Habit 1).

Another key tool for developing your mission statement is your circle of influence. Specifically, the very core of what you have influence over. That core is you and your self-awareness. Your ability to be more loving. To be more productive. To be a better listener. Your ability to understand others without judging them.

Before you have anything else, you have to have self-security. This is your sense of worth and identity. It is a big part of the paradigm that you live in. Your paradigm is the strength of your wisdom. Your mission statement must also have words that you draw guidance from, which are your values. From these you derive your "power" or effectiveness that increases your larger circle of influence that grows from your interdependence with others.

The four cornerstones of your mission statement are:

1. Security

2. Guidance

3. Wisdom

4. Power (effectiveness)

None of these stands alone. Like your interdependence with others, the core elements of your mission statement are interlinked to make you a complete person capable of guiding your fulfilling life. These are the building stones of an integrated person with a character ethic.

Although your mission statement is your bedrock in a changing world, your mission statement is not completely stagnant. The mission statement itself does not need to change; it's the application in your life that will expand as your maturity grows.

Covey has no misgivings that all individuals are at different stages in their development of a guiding mission statement. His process for finding your place in your core development is:

> *"Your security lies somewhere on the continuum between extreme insecurity on one end, wherein your life is buffeted by all the fickle forces that play upon it, and a deep sense of high intrinsic worth and personal security on the other end. Your guidance ranges on the continuum from dependence on the social mirror or other unstable, fluctuating sources to strong inner direction. Your wisdom falls somewhere between a totally inaccurate map where everything is distorted and nothing seems to fit, and a complete and accurate map of life wherein all the parts and principles are properly related to each other. Your power lies somewhere between immobilization or being a puppet pulled by someone else's strings to high proactivity, the power to act according to your own values instead of being acted upon by other people and circumstances."* – Stephen Covey

As you develop your personal mission statement, be determined to firmly place your principles at the center. It's tempting and easy to center it on something that has a special importance for us today. These include highly important dimensions of our lives such as marriage, work, money, parenting, and even religion. These are your values. While none of these should be discounted, the point of a mission statement is enabling you to effectively balance all of the important elements of your life. The center or fulcrum of the balance are your principles.

Your principles won't divorce you nor will they fire you from a job nor can they be destroyed by fire. Your principles are everlasting regardless of anything that happens or changes in your life.

Writing your mission statement is not something that you can do in a single afternoon. It takes considerable introspection just to begin. You'll find that you begin changing as a person as you work through this. Most people will take days, weeks, and even months to complete a first draft. Your mission statement should never be written and then hidden in a desk drawer to collect dust. Some people review their mission statement at the beginning of each new day. Others review it as they plan next week's schedule. And others find a monthly or quarterly review to be enough. As you begin writing your mission statement, frequent reviews are helpful when accompanied by allowing enough time to make revisions until you are fully satisfied that you have captured the words that you can live with the rest of your life.

But before you begin your mission statement, go back to the vision of your own funeral. Begin with the end in mind.

Chapter 3: Transitioning From Visioning to Living a New Life (First Things First)

Habit 3 is the last of the habits that work on you as a person to make you a highly effective individual. Habit 1 is the realization that you are probably not living the life that you envision for yourself. That you are dependent on the life script that has been given to you by others. But that you have everything that you need to change to become an independent person that can evolve to interact interdependently with others.

Habit 2 is the first of the two creations required to accomplish your independence. This is the visualization and definition of who you are becoming. Habit 3 is the implementation or actualization of the vision you create in Habit 2. You cannot implement Habit 2 without first comprehending Habit 1 and you cannot implement Habit 3 without first implementing Habit 2. The sequence cannot be changed nor can any habit be skipped. One follows another, follows another.

Only after you have this foundation are you ready to begin managing your life to be more effective. Even now, your focus remains on making yourself a more effective individual. Although you have an understanding of your circle of influence, you remain limited to first growing your own effectiveness. Improving inner effectiveness is needed before you can improve your effective interactions through interdependence with others.

Habit 3 is the management of your principle-based life. These are the day-to-day behaviors and actions emerging and taking root now that you are on the "right" path in life. With Habit 3, you must fully develop your "Independent Will." This is taking action rather than being acted upon. Taking actions based on what you have become through Habits 1 and 2. It includes keeping commitments and accepting responsibility for your actions because you are living the character ethic.

Independent-will does require self-will power. Something some people believe is lacking in themselves. Will power may be dormant but it is not lacking. You only need to refer back to the human-will power of the many people that have expanded the human experience that found new ways of government, immigrated to new continents, and found new frontiers in space. Strong independent-will power is found in astonishing people like the deaf and blind Helen Keller who accomplished more in her life than most people who possess all of their senses.

Your independent-will is rooted in your principles of honor, integrity, and self-worth. To those principles, you want to add self-discipline. What you do in Habit 3 is to move your principles from thoughts and concepts into **everyday actions**.

Management is about organization, prioritization, and using time wisely. It is about taking planned steps (based on principles) to work towards a goal. In this case, the big goal is a character ethic. Human history is all about improvements evolving one-step at a time. On the highest scale, it is about prehistoric man evolving from hunters and gathers into organized agriculture. The prioritization was feeding themselves and the time management was the seasons of the year. Social groups (living on farms) was the next step. Agriculture innovation followed that and industrialization brought us modern agriculture. Today, we have the information age. None of this would have happened without human will, organization, prioritization, and time management.

Prioritization comes from your values. These are the goals you most want to accomplish. Clearly, you should always make time for your priorities. Yet, many of us become caught up in daily activities and put our priorities on a back burner. Other people become so involved with priorities that they allow everything else in their lives to slide such as relationships and health. Relationships, health, and many parts of your life are truly important but do not receive enough attention when your time is spent doing all of the little things in life.

Priorities and Time Management

Covey developed a very effective model for us to manage both time and priorities. Simple categories can be used for time management. Every time-consuming activity in your life falls into one of these four categories:

1. Urgent and important

2. Not urgent but important

3. Urgent but not important

4. Not urgent and not important

It's a very simple model. You only need to decide how urgent and important anything is to get done. What gets the most attention are things that are both urgent and important. This is how most people prioritize their life but seldom is this the correct priority. The next thing most people spend their time on are what they find to be urgent but not important. The flaw is that "urgent" is not always the top priority.

After the urgent things are finished, most people try to find time to work on what is not urgent but is important. Because our time is so limited, almost all of our time is spent on what is urgent and only when there is time remaining do people get to what is important.

Your mission and values should be your priorities but they are seldom the most urgent matters needing attention. That places your life mission and values in the second category of being "not urgent but important." When you have your priorities wrong, you first work on what is "urgent but not important."

Examples of working on urgent but not important instead of not urgent but important happens constantly throughout the days of most people. A telephone that rings while you are working on your mission statement is a good example. The ringing of the telephone makes it urgent but the fact that it is an unwanted sales pitch makes it not important. What happens is you answer the urgent telephone but it interrupts working on your mission statement. Your mission statement is much more important but it doesn't seem as urgent as the ringing telephone.

You do need to spend time in all four of the categories but it's critical to manage your time by spending the most time working on the "urgent and important" followed by the "not urgent but important." Considerably less of your time should be dedicated to "urgent but not important" and "not urgent and not important."

Urgent and important are things like taking care of a medical emergency as well as going to work to earn a living to support yourself and your family. Not urgent but important is working on your mission statement but also day-to-day activities that involve your values like taking the time to practice good parenting skills.

Urgent but not important probably takes up much more of your time than it should. These are the ringing telephones that don't need to be answered or the supplier at work that shows up unexpectedly to show you his new line of products. These are things that can be postponed and once postponed often lose the urgency. Or sometimes these can be delegated to someone else (interdependency). And there are the things that are "not urgent and not important." Most of these can be eliminated but not all of them. Relaxing in front of the TV, reading a book for pleasure, and other types of recreation might seem to be "not urgent and not important." However, we need these in our lives as an opportunity to recharge our minds and batteries without a constant onslaught of other stimulation.

There are two important things to keep in mind when organizing, prioritizing, and managing your time. First, be sure you are prioritizing correctly. Many people make a mistake of categorizing items that are really "urgent but not important" into the category of "urgent and important." These people spend almost all of their time working on what they think is both urgent and important. When they are finally exhausted, they shift their little remaining time to "not urgent and not important" so that they can get some rest and relaxation. What becomes neglected is "not urgent but important" which is where your mission statement and values fall. Correctly prioritizing your activities is critical to time management.

The second important thing to keep in mind is time allocation. The people that are the least effective are those who spend most of their time on what is "urgent but not important" and "not urgent and not important." Highly effective people spend most of their time with what is "urgent and important" and "not urgent but important." You need to spend your time in all four categories but most time needs to be spent on what is important. You also need to be sure you are allocating enough time on "not urgent but important" and much less time on "urgent but not important."

When it comes to priorities and time management, keep the Pareto Principle in mind – 80% of the results flow out of 20% of the activities. You should spend at least 20% of your time on your mission statement related activities.

A good exercise at this point is to find at least one thing (personal or professional) that if you spent more time on would make a significant difference in your life. Finding more time for this is a good start to Habit 3.

Having Priorities Means Knowing When to Say No or Yes

As your effectiveness and circle of influence increases, so will your opportunities to be involved with urgent and important activities. You will have to learn how to say no to some of these.

Think about your typical day and how many times you say yes or no to many different opportunities. Is your response usually based on a gut reaction? Do you reflexively say no because you are too busy with something else but just as reflexively say yes when the request comes from your boss or someone else with authority? These are reactive rather than proactive responses.

Saying either yes or no without contemplation means you have not fully embraced Habit 2. You are not weighing your decision against your **mission statement, principles**, and **values**. This involves leadership coming before management. First, decide what the right thing to do is and then decide how to get it done. It also has a lot in common with time management. You want to do what is important and then decide how urgent it is. You might say yes to do something but at a different time or in a way that requires less time. What you do should be based on your priorities that are driven by your principles and values.

If the request is not a good fit, your inclination should be to say no but say it with respect. No is typically said along the lines of, "you have a very good idea that needs to be done and I appreciate you asking me to be part of the solution. However, because of time limitations and other priorities, I won't be able to participate." With a boss, you might want to politely ask him or her to join you in looking over all of the other priority assignments that you have to help decide which ones to postpone or cancel. There are many polite ways of saying no that show respect to the person making the request.

Before you say yes, you need tools to make the decision. First and foremost, you should have your mission statement available so that you can be sure there is no conflict. Even when it is a good fit, you still need to manage your busy schedule. Covey uses the word "coherence" to describe what to look for when taking on new tasks. Beyond your mission statement, it should fit with the goals you are currently working towards or offer a stepping-stone toward a future goal. It could be a short- or long-term goal that determines the timeline the task fits in. If it fits with a short-term goal, your decision should still include your priorities and other plans. If it fits long-term, it might be a placeholder that does not require additional evaluation at the current time.

When you have a mission statement, values, and principles that are organized and prioritized, you have the management tools to decide when to say yes or no and when to commit to completing tasks. Another tool to use is the sense of maintaining balance among your values such as marriage, work, money, parenting, and recreation.

You should take time to regularly reflect on your activities and make changes as needed. A daily "to-do" list can be a good management tool but you need to step into a leadership role also. The week is a measurement of time that severs society well. Work, school, and family schedules revolve around weekly schedules.

Before beginning each new week, you serve yourself well by reflecting on the coming week's activities and making changes or adjustments using the tools you now have in your toolbox. One way to do this is by reviewing each weekly activity against your mission statement and goals, as well as prioritizing them into the four categories for urgency and importance. You should also regularly schedule time to review long term goals.

Living Your Independent Will

When you implement Habit 3 to follow your independent-will, your life will stop being controlled by impulsive decisions and actions. You will no longer come to the end of a day, week, or month and wonder if your efforts had any real meaning. Although not everything you do will be principle driven beyond reason, you will feel accomplishment on a daily and frequent basis.

But don't become too hung up on "efficiency." Not everything in life can be scheduled. This is particularly true when other people are involved. There will be times when a husband, wife, or other important person needs more of your time than usual or that you have planned for. These are times when you need to have flexibility. These are times when one particular value needs more of your time and attention than your other values.

Part Three: PLAYING AND WORKING WELL WITH OTHERS

Only after you are satisfied with your forward momentum toward independent-will as the inner person you want to be, can you be highly effective at Interdependence with others. Moving towards better interdependence begins from where you are now. You should have a new map to guide you where you are now going in life but the fact is that your old map has placed you where you are today. You can change where you are going but you can't change where you are beginning from.

You have relationships with people today that you almost certainly want to keep while going forward. You want to change those relationships based on your new maturity but these relationships have a history. You cannot change the fundamentals of those relationships simply by telling people that you have had an awakening and are now living a meaningful life based on a new paradigm. First of all, these people have not had an awakening or paradigm shift. If you're lucky, some of these people will already have a character ethic and live a life based on principles and interdependency. But most of them are not likely to yet be on the path you have chosen.

Remember, you've had a fundamental paradigm shift. If you have any doubts about where you are at right now, go back and revisit the first three habits that are at the root of your new paradigm. Interdependence and your new self-fulfilling life can now become the trunk, branches, leaves, and fruit of your life tree. There is still a lot of growth to be accomplished. Now is the time to **walk the talk**.

Being proactive, you begin interacting with others based on principles, values, and putting integrity first. Always remember that throughout your entire life you will still be learning. This is only a beginning with the end in mind. Your earliest goals are building rich, enduring, effective, and productive relationships.

Something to look out for is digressing back into personality ethic techniques. Character ethics are based on full interdependence that includes all interactions. It is not based on quick fixes and temporary band aids.

Building Trust Based Relationships

An important analogy that Covey uses are financial bank accounts because we all understand that we need to deposit at least as much money as we withdraw or we'll go bankrupt. He applies this analogy to relationships by replacing money with emotions. As you begin this life changing evolution, you need to be prepared to make more deposits into relationships than you make withdrawals. Depending on your past, or where you are beginning from, you may need to make substantial deposits before considering making any withdrawals. You may even be starting with a negative emotional account.

This begins with keeping your commitments, which are at the heart of your integrity and self-worth. Along with your commitments, you want to show respect for others while being honest and kind. Building trust is essential, especially in the beginning. All of this leads to better communication that would otherwise be hindered by broken commitments and lack of honesty.

When trust levels are low, you might be able to temporarily keep a relationship on life support by living mutually independent lives that avoid conflict by avoiding interactions (or stepping on each other's toes). But this is an unsustainable relationship that will grow apart. In other situations, it will rise to open warfare causing any facade of an effective relationship to cease abruptly. Establishing and building trust is essential.

Not all relationships are the same nor do all of them require the same amount of attention. All relationships need to be based on trust but the effort required to establish and maintain trust is different in different relationships. Generally, the more time spent in a relationship, the more effort you need to make towards supporting it and maintaining trust. For most people, these are marriages and nuclear family relationships. If you are in the workforce, those people are included, as are close friends, and others that you will need to identify.

There are also times when a new relationship needs extra attention developing trust and communication that will require less effort once it is established. And there are old relationships where encounters are seldom. A rule of thumb governing old and passed relationships is that these pick up where they last left off. If trust was established, trust will still exist. If trust was lacking, it will need to be rebuilt. An example is an ex-spouse that you share parenting responsibilities with. If the old relationship disintegrated into distrust, the person's trust will need to be earned again. If there was no break in the trust, the interdependent relationship can be made stronger more quickly.

The best first step is **listening to understand** the other person. Don't offer (and certainly don't force) your advice or tell them what you would do. Just listen to understand. You can ask how or why they made a decision but don't question their logic or try to make them understand why you would have done something different. Life is full of opportunities to simply listen and just as full of temptation to offer to solve a person's problem when they don't even consider it a problem. In a simple context, this might be listening to why your husband wants to buy a boat for the approaching summer season when you don't think it can be afforded financially. First listen to understand and nothing else. Questions might be along the line of asking why the unexpected interest in boating. You can even make a positive deposit in the relationship account by picking up a boating magazine to help build a damaged relationship or to improve a healthy interdependent relationship.

Listening to build trust might seem counterproductive if you have little trust for the other person. But that lack of trust is a symptom of a damaged relationship. If you first jump in by offering advice and objecting to their actions or behaviors, you will only damage the relationship further. If you want to save and improve the relationship, you must take action to build trust. That begins by understanding what the other person is thinking or why they are behaving the way that they are. Just telling them that they are wrong and to change will get you nowhere and will probably further deteriorate the relationship.

Listening to understand is only the first of the six major deposits needing to be made into interdependent relationships. But understanding leads to being able to effectively make the other types of deposits. You first have to understand what others value the most as a deposit and to be aware when their perceptions or values change. That's not a change in a core value but a change in what is important at the time. Returning to the boating example, picking up a magazine may seem trivial to a husband who would much more value an invitation to spend time on a friend's boat or to visit a marina. That would be a huge emotional deposit. You might not fall in love with boating but you will demonstrate your love for your husband.

This is where **courtesy and respect for others** comes in as the second type of deposit into the relationship account. Through first understanding the other person, you learn what little things they most appreciate. For example, in these times when women are finding ways to better assert their rights, knowing whether or not to open a car door for a woman can be challenging for men. Most men do this as a sign of respect and even affection and some women appreciate it that way. However, other women find it shows disrespect by ignoring their own capabilities and self-worth. You have to first understand the person before you can show meaningful and effective small courtesies.

Still, showing respect and small courtesies can be very important if the relationship is damaged or if trust is low. You want to combine this with living up to your **commitment**s, which is another of the six major deposits.

Fulfilling commitments is based on expectations and expectations often require clarification. **Clarifying expectations** is a form of understanding but also has its own merits as a deposit in the relationship account. Clarifying expectations is particularly important in both a new relationship and when an existing relationship encounters a new situation. It can also be important when an existing situation changes. It's best to clarify expectations early when commitments are being made. Commitments can be both actions and behaviors. Clear expectations can vary greatly. A man that has a behavior of ogling women in public may see this as harmless. Whereas a woman in a relationship may see this as a great disrespect. Other women might see this as acceptable male behavior except when he is with another woman, especially a woman he is romantically involved with. Clarifying some expectations can be difficult but also critical to avoiding serious and even irreparable damage to a relationship.

Last but not the least of the major deposits is **your integrity**. Integrity is about living and behaving in the way that we tell others what we believe. Integrity is walking the talk. Do you tell your wife that you love her, respect her, and make the effort to show her small courtesies? And then tell people at work that she constantly nags you? That would lack integrity. Your love for her and her nagging you might even be reality. But complaining about her to others would be disrespectful. Not only is it disrespectful but it causes others to wonder what you say about them behind their back. Lack of integrity destroys trust. Showing loyalty for those who are not present is one of the most important ways of showing integrity to build trust. Integrity is about treating everyone by the same set of principles.

Integrity and honesty are intertwined and easily confused. You can honestly tell someone the facts in a way that causes an incorrect understanding. It's the old adage that "liars figure and figures lie." Integrity is presenting the facts both honestly and accurately. It includes clarifying that your opinion is involved when it is.

Sooner or later, you will make withdrawals from any meaningful relationship account. You will say or do something damaging to the relationship. Hopefully this happens when you already have a positive balance in the account. Apologizing minimizes the withdrawal and damage. The sooner you realize what you have done wrong and make a sincere apology, the less damage it causes. If you discover you have betrayed someone's confidence or made a mistake, apologize for it as soon as possible. Even before the other person discovers what you've done wrong. That is integrity in a difficult or uncomfortable situation. An apology can even turn into a deposit when it is done with integrity. On the other hand, repeated apologies, especially for the same behavior, become larger withdrawals each time.

Only after you understand and internalize the value of relationship deposits are you ready to begin the habits of interdependence. The remaining four habits create effective interdependence; first within your circle of influence and then to expand your circle.

Chapter 4: Win-Win Without Compromise (Think Win-Win)

Compromise flows from competition. Win-win flows from cooperation. Compromise almost always results in one person getting more than the other does. Sometimes, compromise even means this time you get your way and next time, I get my way.

A win-win solution means we all get what we want. Win-win requires a paradigm shift in how we seek solutions. It's not a perfect world and not every solution will be perfect but at least you can start from a paradigm where everyone wins.

Alternatively, you can have win-lose, lose-win, lose-lose, or take no action. All except for the last one are forms of compromise. It's only with win-win that everyone involved is fully committed to taking the action agreed to.

Changing to a win-win paradigm can be particularly difficult for people operating from a position of power. They have become used to giving directions, conceding on a minor point of objection, and then ordering his or her directions to be carried out. These people believe conceding on a minor point to be a compromise and then wonder why their orders aren't carried out with enthusiasm and cooperation.

Win-lose and lose-win scenarios only work when trust is not needed or not present. About the only time these make sense is in a purely competitive situation such as a foot race. The entire point of the situation is to have a winner and a loser. But that doesn't mean a win-lose paradigm applies to all (or even many) competitive scenarios. Take a need at work to come up with the best presentation and concepts for a new client. You could have several people show the boss their best presentation and pick a winner from among the competing presentations. But this would not best serve the client. Instead, the best from all presentations should be offered to the prospective client as a representation of what you can accomplish through cooperation. Often this expands (synergy) to improving on the best of the best.

Win-win is interdependent rather than independent. You'll be much more effective through cooperation than through competition.

Lose-win is the worst of the scenarios because it is fully dependent. People who are completely dependent on others expect to lose and accept losing without standing up for themselves. The only way this scenario can get any worse is when the person the loser is dependent on takes full advantage of the dependent person. Even people with low morals and principles find this behavior despicable. Both of the people in lose-win scenarios lack self-esteem and will not find fulfilment in life.

Lose-lose is typically the result of two people with a win-lose paradigm trying to work together. Both are so consumed with getting "one-up" on the other that nothing useful results from their efforts. This could be confused with a "take no action" paradigm except that a lot of effort goes into getting nothing done.

A take no action result is better than a lose-lose because the energy can be used elsewhere. Also, the two people involved come away without animosity. They may not be able to work together this time but they can agree to work together on a future project.

There are situations for each of these alternatives but you need to think long and hard about the consequences before using them. Win-lose does work when the point is having a competition that doesn't require cooperation. Besides the footrace, in business this can work when different regions of a business are competing to bring in new clients as long as they aren't competing for the same clients. There are times when the importance of a relationship can make a lose-win result the best choice. This requires a relationship that is already strong and based on trust. Lose-win works when the person losing doesn't care about winning and is more concerned about making a deposit to the relationship.

When the relationship is interdependent, the win-win scenario is almost always preferred. In any ongoing relationship, any other scenario is almost certain to create hard feelings. You may win one time but not in the long term. Try running the different scenarios against any situation in your life. If you truly consider the probable outcomes, the win-win paradigm is the right paradigm. Win-win is where the synergy is at – interdependence.

When win-win can't be achieved, taking no action becomes the other best alternative. No expectations have been created and neither has tried to out manipulate the other. You've actually reached an agreement that you can't work together on this project.

What Goes into Win-Win

Learning to be effective at win-win comes after your inner work at becoming self-aware, exercising your imagination, conscience, and independence. Everything from the first three habits goes into your win-win paradigm.

You need integrity to accomplish win-win. Without integrity, it becomes easy to allow others to become the loser. You also need your values so that you can define what winning means to you in all situations. You need to be able to keep your commitments; otherwise there is no point in even finding a win-win solution.

You need the maturity to understand the needs of others and that these are as important as your own needs. This is respect and empathy for others. Maturity is the ability to look for long term results rather than instant gratification. It is understanding that meaningful interdependent relationships need to stand the test of time.

Win-win also requires that you believe there is enough to go around for everyone. You need to think that by you getting your way doesn't mean someone else has to go without. The solution isn't dividing a small pie; the solution is creating a bigger pie. This is an abundance for all. The opposite of abundance is scarcity. Your paradigm needs to be one of abundance. You also have to accept that others have the right to the same amount as you. This is about moving from competition to cooperation. Self-worth fits here as confidence that you'll receive what you need.

When you play and work well with others, you don't have a need or desire to manipulate or dominate them. Instead, it means gladly sharing credit and recognition with others for accomplishments and solutions. Developing a win-win paradigm can be very difficult for people deeply immersed in a win-lose paradigm. If you have trouble, there is plenty of literature that you might want to read for examples. Some are autobiographies and some is fiction such as Chariots of Fire or Les Miserables.

Relationships Thrive with Win-Win

Finding win-win answers is one of the best ways to make deposits in relationship accounts. This is particularly effective after you have established trust. Win-win answers demonstrated that you value long term interdependent relationships. On the other hand, even if you have demonstrated honesty and established trust, working towards win-lose or the other alternatives shows a lack of respect for the relationship going forward.

Beginning a new relationship with a person in the win-win paradigm can be particularly challenging. Beyond explaining the paradigm to them, it requires building the trust and respect already discussed. This is almost always going to require more communication than needed for an existing relationship or when beginning a new relationship with a person who already understands and strives for a win-win solution. That begins by first listening to understand the other person, which is also the starting point with existing relationships. More communication and time are what make the difference depending on where the relationship is beginning from. But since win-win is a self-evident principle almost everyone will come to embrace it when given time and respect.

Agreements flow from win-win proposals and solutions. Agreements flow into responsibilities and actionable commitments. None of this is going to happen if you or others aren't committed to the entire solution. Proposals and solutions are desired outcomes. Guidelines for actions are based on values and principles. Resources such as money and physical equipment are often needed to make actions possible. And there needs to be accountability that measures the results based on the guidelines and desired results. Without the desired results being clearly defined, you have no way of knowing when the win-win solution has been completed or accomplished. The good news is that win-win creates an incredible synergy that achieves mutually agreed to results much faster and with fewer resources than any of the other paradigms.

When you have leadership and management responsibilities, win-win will thrive when it is aligned with the reward system. If you have a reward system only for winners, it encourages everyone involved to follow a win-lose paradigm. Core to the win-win paradigm is that everyone can be rewarded when everyone contributes to the achieving the desired results. If the reward system only rewards two out of ten participants, you'll miss out on the synergy of the other eight participants. Even if you convince everyone to fully participate the first time, the results will be diminished the next time. On the other hand, if everyone wins, his or her enthusiasm will increase the next time – assuming you've built trust that this is the paradigm that will be rewarded. To create a reward system that works, you must first understand the people involved and what motivates them. Cooperation is highly effective even when the odds are stacked against them. Win-win solutions come from win-win rewards and processes.

Chapter 5 – Effective Communication (Seek First to Understand and Then to Be Understood)

Listening, talking, reading, and writing are the basic forms of communication. Think about how much time you spend engaged in one of these forms of communication every day. Include listening to the TV or radio because these also are conveying messages to you. Almost everything you do during your waking hours involves communication.

Your fundamental education goes deep into learning how to read and write. It begins with the alphabet the first year you go to school. Then you learn how to read words and write sentences. You learn the different parts of sentences and how to use grammar. All of that is just to get you started with reading and writing. In secondary school and college, you read textbooks and write reports constantly. All of this is to prepare you for all of the communication that you will be involved with for the rest of your life. But.......

How much time do you spend learning how to LISTEN??

Not much time is dedicated to learning to listen. You might take a specialized course in communication but most of it will be about presenting your own ideas to be better understood. You can probably see where this is going. All of us need a lot more practice at listening, especially learning how to listen effectively. An alternative title to this habit is "Listening Effectively Before Communicating."

Listening First to Understand

Listening to understand is another paradigm shift for most people. Anything you have to say has much more effect when you put it into the perspective that the other person understands. That requires you first understand the perspective that the other person has.

Most people make no attempt to listen to understand the other person. People listen to find a point where they can interject their thoughts or experiences. And they listen to decide how to form their reply. Often that reply is a rebuttal to what the other person is saying or how they would do things differently. All without first understanding the other person's perspective of why they did something or why they think a certain way.

Have you ever heard a father say that he doesn't understand his kids or that kids don't understand their parents? Of course, they don't because they haven't listened to the other's perspective. Today's kids didn't grow up during the cold war and today's parents weren't nearly as bombarded with information as today's kids are in the advanced information age. Both are communicating to be understood and neither is listening to first understand the other.

This isn't limited to parents and children. The same thing goes on in the workplace, in houses of worship, when interpreting movies, in navigating relationships, and every other aspect of life. In fact, most of us have the same reply to the same situation for everyone that we communicate with – all from the focus of our own perspective.

There are roughly four listening styles. First is simply ignoring what the other person is saying. This could be simply understanding the main topic is baseball and replying about the last game we saw when the other person was talking about the rules of the game. Second is pretending to listen by nodding your head at the right time while formulating what you are going to say next. A third is selective listening when we listen just enough to pick out one of many subjects that we want to reply to. Even active listening has limitations. It resembles selective listening when we actively listen to pick out words and phrases that we relate to. At the higher end, active listening is repeating back (paraphrasing) what we heard. But active listening still lacks perspective.

None of those is **empathic listening**. Only at this highest level do we listen to put everything into context of the other person's perspective. When we actually do this, our reply and interaction is more likely to be a question for clarification or for more information rather than a reply about our own experiences and thoughts on the subject. This is the new paradigm.

Empathic listening goes far beyond just understanding the words being spoken. It requires completely understanding all of the communication. Experts estimate that 90% of what is being communicated comes from body language and how we say things. The actual words only communicate 10% of the message. How we say things includes inflection points like saying "you know" and adding an "hmm…" between words or thoughts. Inflections and body language is where you get the "feeling" of what is being communicated.

Effective communication, beginning with listening to understand, plays a big role towards making deposits in a relationship account. It can make the difference between the interaction being a deposit or a withdrawal. Withdrawals happen when the other person views your actions and words as being used against them to manipulate, intimidate, or cause another negative emotional outcome. On the other hand, empathic listening strengthens a relationship when the person knows they are both being listened to and understood. It's almost therapeutic in some situations. It makes the person feel validated.

Much of what you have already read goes into empathetic listening. First, it doesn't bring on the instant gratification that you would get if you assume how smart you are by thinking you know the answer before understanding the question. But it does increase your circle of influence when people come to trust that you understand from their perspective. It also opens you up to being influenced by others.

Empathetic listening is necessary in all parts of life. When a salesman listens to understand the customer's needs, he can recommend the right product that meets the customer's needs. Only hearing that the customer is looking for a TV might lead a salesman to emphasize the features of the biggest screen when the customer needs something small to fit into his small den. You don't want a lawyer recommending divorce when you go to him looking for a solution to evict your husband's deadbeat brother from the guest room. And you don't want a real estate agent selling you a seaside cabin when you want something in the woods. You need others to listen to what you need rather than telling you what they have to offer.

Start practicing empathetic listening by first understanding what you are listening for. Are you listening to decide to agree or disagree or are you listening to gather information without making a judgement? Do you ask probing questions to understand how the other person is feeling or do you tell the other person how they should feel?

Although first listening to understand isn't the place to start practicing the seven habits, it is often the place where people want to start because they perceive it can be the easiest place to start. There's nothing wrong with starting here but the synergy is more powerful when you first change the paradigms about yourself.

Active listening (which isn't actually a higher form of listening) does play a role in empathetic listening. It makes sure that you did hear the words correctly and it tells the speaker that you at least heard them. However, if you haven't already established that you have a character ethic and established trust, it can sound condescending to the speaker. When you do repeat back what you heard, do two things. Beyond just paraphrasing, put the meaning of what you heard into your own words. That tells the other person that you are thinking about what they said even if you don't get the meaning correct. When you follow this with a question for the other person to explain further, you encourage them to open up more. They will only do this if they have trust in you. The more the person opens up, the more context you have to possibly provide meaningful solutions or another way of thinking about it. Very possibly, you'll come upon ideas that you never would have thought of if you didn't have the correct context.

But don't be too quick to offer a solution or advice. Often just opening up and putting their problem or situation into words enables the other person to arrive at their own correct solution. This takes a lot of good judgement on your part because there will be times when the person is specifically looking for your advice. The more information you have, the better advice you will be able to give. As you and the other person go deeper and deeper to find the root of the problem, the answer can come to either of you at any time. What's important is that both of you understand that you have found the root of the problem.

Still, those are only tools for listening to understand. There is no substitute for you having a genuine desire to understand the perspective of others. That desire begins with the first three habits. For instance, if you get a person to open up and, in the end, you make a commitment to that person that you don't follow through on; you will do more damage in the form of a relationship withdrawal than you accomplished by practicing empathetic listening skills.

You Want to Be Understood

First, you need to understand that your perceptions are not facts, just as another person's perceptions are not facts. Your own perception can change daily and hourly. If you just finished paying the household bills when your child comes to you asking for a raise in his or her allowance, you're likely to begin with a very different perception about the value of money than if he or she came to you on payday and right after taking care of all his or her chores. It all depends on how you are looking at the world at a given moment.

And you've had paradigms for years that are the foundation of your perceptions. What's important is knowing that perceptions are not facts. No one "sees the facts" the same way that you see them. It's your ability to understand the facts from multiple perspectives that makes you a more effective person. It is different perspectives that find different resources to help solve problems and to get things done.

You also want to be understood but there is a sequence that makes this work best. Especially when dealing with a person that has no understanding of the *7 Habits of Highly Effective People*. That sequence is your character, your relationships, and then your logic. Each build on the other so that your perspective can be understood.

For most people it seems intuitive to begin with the logic and then explain how you arrived at it. However, when people trust your character and trust the relationship, the logic becomes much easier to understand. How you go about being understood is another paradigm shift.

You being understood begins by first understanding others. Acknowledge what they want to accomplish and acknowledge their concerns. This means that what they want and their concerns have to be directly addressed by the logic you are offering. If your logic doesn't match, they won't be able to understand what you are trying to communicate. Even if you have the same goal, if your logic doesn't work for their concerns, you won't be able to develop the synergy of interdependence. **First, seek to understand and then seek to be understood.**

Developing effective communication skills solves most of the problems that you will encounter. It can help you find resources that you need, it can correct unacceptable behavior, it gets to the root of what matters, it resolves disagreements, it makes you appreciate others more, it makes you more respectful of others, it changes circumstances, it makes problems go away, and it increases your circle of influence.

Chapter 6 – The Merging of Synergy (Synergy)

The purpose of synergy is to bring all of the other habits together for the purpose of maximizing your effectiveness through interdependence. At the heart of synergy are win-win solutions and empathetic listening. This is how alternatives are first envisioned and then enacted. Without the other habits, these alternatives would almost certainly go undiscovered.

Synergy is simple to understand. Synergy is when the combined efforts of several people achieve more than the total of what each individual can accomplish alone. Another way of thinking about this is that relationships create a third power between two people and multiple relationships far exceed the individual capabilities and capacity of each person. Increased creativity is an example of one of these increases in power. Two brains are better than one and when one person's creativity builds on the creativity of another, a third level of creativity is reached.

People shy away from synergy for several reasons. Among these is fear of the unknown because neither is in direct control of the results. And yet, exploring the unknown is the key characteristic of pioneers and trailblazers that lead the way for others.

Nature and man-made creations are good examples of synergy. Among the greatest man-made synergy creations is the building of skyscrapers from cement and steel. Nature combines rain, soil, and seeds to grow an abundance of plant life. The world is much fuller of examples of what synergy can create than it is of solo accomplishments.

Humans can only maximize synergy when they share freely rather than guarding the little they have. It's an abundance mentality. Rather than being guarded and defensive, synergy requires being open to new possibilities and new alternatives. Synergy is an alternative to being selfish. If you've never experienced synergy, it is because you've never allowed it as an alternative way of thinking, behaving, and working. Sports team spirit or taking group action in an emergency are easy examples to understand. These are times when people naturally work together without giving it direct thought.

Creative Synergy

Synergy is a simple three-step process. Trusting relationships must exist or be developed before people will open up. Part of the process is learning and understanding the paradigms of others. This includes their background, hopes, and concerns. It requires an openness not easily achieved in many business relationships and sadly not even in some family relationships. One sign that synergy is being achieved is when disagreements become opportunities to better understand the other side rather to defend your own position. Another indicator that occurs in business settings is when participants are more interested in upholding the spirit of an agreement rather than the letter of a contract.

Most people are mature enough to show respect to others. They don't regularly take defensive positions without acknowledging the right of others to have an opinion. However, in the middle respective position (defensive – respective - synergetic), people focus mostly on decorum with polite language, giving others the time to express opinions, and acknowledging the intelligence of others. But this is done without giving serious consideration to how another position can be a better alternative and lacks exploring how multiple alternatives can be melded into a truly synergistic alternative. This common type of respective behavior allows all positions to be heard and then one position to "win" in the end. The result is a lack of enthusiasm and commitment by the many that did not have their idea chosen. Synergy has the opposite result when the best of several ideas are commingled to create a better alternative that many contributed to and many will commit to.

Synergy fits closely with how win-win compares with compromise. Win-win results in everyone getting everything they wanted and often more. Compromise is when everyone gets half of what they wanted and the result is the whole is less than the individual pieces.

Synergy should be uplifting. It increases energy levels and makes experiences more enjoyable. Defensive and purely respective behaviors and thoughts have the opposite effect. These create negative energy defending what shouldn't need to be defended and lower energy from waiting out time while someone else explains a position that we are not openly considering. It is also boring because we are essentially trying to create clones who will think and act exactly as we do. Becoming open to the possibilities of synergy requires that we first become the independent and secure individuals that are created with the first three habits.

Exceeding Your Own Limitations

To be effective, you need to be able to recognize that two people can disagree and both of them are still right. It happens all of the time when two people are given the samet facts or circumstances but come to two different and equally logical conclusions. Synergy requires that you be able to **value these differences.** You have to first agree that both responses are correct.

For example, one spouse in a marriage is given a pay raise that both earned because one took care of the majority of the household so that the other could pursue a career. One wants to save the additional money for a future need. The other wants to spend the money as a reward for hard work and postponing gratification. Which one is right? Does that mean the other one is wrong?

Instead of spending your time trying to convince others to see things your way, ask them to explain why they see things their way. Even if you never come to an agreement, you will have learned something. Something that you may find valuable in this or another situation.

There isn't much value in explaining your position to someone who already agrees with you. That's why it's called preaching to the choir. The value comes from communicating with people that think differently from you. People who have the same facts as you but arrive at a different conclusion. Two wrongs don't make a right but two rights do make synergy.

Synergy Overcomes Negative Forces

Negative forces and negative people exist. You will encounter them. Often you can't exactly describe what those negative forces are. There is just a negative feeling in a room, a relationship, or an organization. You might describe it as not feeling safe to express yourself or being restrained from saying what is on your mind. These are real forces from emotional, illogical, unconscious, and social powers.

For a while, you can use many of the 7 habits you have learned to overpower these negative powers. You do this with respect, openness, and honesty. But these alone are not always enough to permanently overcome emotional and illogical powers. What you need to permanently reduce or stop the negative powers is to engage the participants in a synergistic activity. You want to first get them to see the problem as others see it and then work towards a synergistic solution. This uses all of the habits from part two of the book - motive from Habit 4, the skills from Habit 5, and the interaction from Habit 6. This transforms negative forces into positive forces that increase the effectiveness of everyone involved. The negative forces are not just put on pause; the experience weakens and eliminates the negativity.

The preferred outcome is new and shared goals. Goals that everyone works towards enthusiastically. Common goals that people can be reminded of if old negative behaviors reemerge.

This is about an old culture being transformed into a new culture. It is not about changing the rules of the negative culture to be fairer. It's about creating new rules that everyone wants to play by because no one was winning with the negative rules. No single person creates the new rules. Synergy is used to build upon the suggestions of everyone. It's about a win-win solution that everyone feels good about. This is how synergy creates a paradigm shift in an entire organization, or family, or relationship.

Habit 6 is the accumulation and application of the other five habits. When someone disagrees with you, take it as an opportunity to learn about another perspective and make something new and better from the effort. Disagreements are the beginning for finding an alternative solution that hadn't been considered.

Part Four:

COMPLETING THE CIRCLE AGAIN AND AGAIN

This is the final and ongoing proactive step. This is about not becoming complacent in the maturity progress that you have achieved. Habit 7 revisits the other 6 habits until they become the center of who we are. Although it revisits all 6 habits, it aligns mostly with habits 1 through 3 based on self-understanding, self-worth, and self-improvement. From a time management view, Habit 7 falls into the category of not urgent but important. You need to plan time in your busy life to refresh what you need to be doing by revisiting the fundamental values that define your lifetime of happiness and success.

Studying and embracing the 7 habits makes you a more effective person. But achieving and maintaining higher effectiveness requires regularly revisiting and reaffirming your principles and values. Habit 7 resembles making it a good practice to frequently refer to your mission statement when making difficult decisions.

Chapter 7: Self-Synergy (Sharpen the Saw)

Covey suggests that part of this renewal includes regular physical exercise, spirituality, expanding mentally (including examination of your own paradigms), and the social/emotional aspects of your life (personal vision, leadership, management, and being self-secure when working with others). Many examples of all four activities are provided by Covey.

Habit 7 is the way we ingrain our daily life with integrity by practicing the other 6 habits to reflect our deepest values. This is also the time and method to keep the habits balanced. A check that you are not overcompensating with one habit while neglecting another. Without balance, all six habits will be negatively impacted and will lose their effectiveness. All six are tightly integrated. As you work on any one of them, it has an effect on the others. For instance, better physical health improves endurance to increase your ability to engage longer and more effectively in the spiritual, mental, and the social/emotional aspects of life. Spiritual growth leads to better leadership, social, and personal interactions that are key to your interdependence. Mental activities increase open-mindedness as well as exposure to other perspectives. Social/emotional self-control brings on more self-security.

The interactions are many. And although balance is the most highly effective, proactive effort in each one provides more awareness in each of the others. This is the synergy of Habit 7. Each time you achieve better consciousness of one habit, the relationship to the other habits becomes clearer. Although the habits must first be learned sequentially, the ultimate value is synergistic application of all six.

Organizational Application

The failing of some (or many) organizations is not achieving balance or even application of all six habits. In the case of business, physical health is a metaphor for making money. There are countless examples where making money is the only purpose of the organization. This encourages many types of negative human characteristics when individuals are only valued for the amount of money they can bring to the organization. Information that should be shared becomes secrets instead. Politics replaces cooperation. Self-defensiveness replaces listening to understand. These go along with many other negative characteristics, all for the sake of making money.

That is not to say that businesses should not make money. They must, in order to survive. But a lack of principles and lack of a sense for serving others is not an effective method of making money. Money seeking alone will create a synergy but it is a negative synergy into a downward spiral.

In business, the spiritual aspect manifests in the need to serve the consumers of its products as well as the community. The need to serve a greater good. It is a realization that the business is the servant and not the master. This is where you find outstanding customer service, loyal customers, and community support.

Mental growth of a business occurs when people are being developed. When talents are valued, rewarded, and people are placed where they are the most effective.

The social/emotional health of a business is shown in the way that it treats people. In the way that all perspectives are encouraged to be expressed, understood, and sincere efforts are made to find win-win solutions.

Just as a singular business-focus on money creates a negative synergy, when a business overcompensates in other areas, it becomes a social experiment that no longer serves a purpose in the business world. Just like individuals, businesses need a soul that develops, renews, and keeps all four in balance. Without these, a business deteriorates into an autocracy where resistance develops from multiple forces. These are places where turnover is chronic, deep cultural divides are the norm, and neither internal nor external loyalty exists.

Aspire to Continuous Improvement

Being truly proactive is vital to highly effective people. Habit 7 is the continuation of being proactive. Awareness of the tools is but a beginning. First applications of the habits will be limited to the easiest questions to answer and easiest situations to resolve. And that is how it should be. It is through continued practice and application toward more difficult circumstances that these news tools become habits woven into the fabric of our lives.

People have been aware for many generations of the value of living purpose driven and principle-based lives. This is the desire of most people. Religions, philosophies, and other higher plains of thinking occupy the center of the human consciousness. Historical and modern examples of people who have achieved this are abundant. Many have shared their thought processes and guiding principles in autobiographies. Few, if any, have presented methods as useful tools the way Covey does. Unused tools turn to rust. Only by continuous use and care of these tools will you continue growing into the person you want to be.

> *"Peace of mind comes when your life is in harmony with true principles and values and in no other way."*
>
> \-   *Stephen Covey*

CONCLUSION

Stephen Covey's 7 Habits of Highly Effective People remains at the pinnacle of self-help books for very good reasons. It is unlike the thousands of other books that have come before and after. Rather than long technical details about the failings and success of human psychology, it provides simple and easy to implement tools that make a tremendous difference in your life. The tools are particularly effective because they become **habits** that we use to continue growing throughout the remainder of our lives.

Life is only beginning once we reach adulthood. To achieve what we want most from life and become all that we can be, we must continue the maturity process to become fully independent adults. This requires creating our own personal map for life based on principles and values that leads to character ethics. This self-realization is the key to mature independence.

Only after we are truly mature individuals are we able to effectively interact with all others that we encounter in life. Covey calls this "interdependence." It is an approach to life where, as individuals, we achieve what we want by working with others to achieve what they want. For many, the concept of creating an abundance for all must replace the concept of that there is not enough for everyone to lead a meaningful life. The key is that when we help others, they help us in return to create a bigger pie that all of us share.

In the end, much of this seems like common sense, which is why it is so easy to begin applying to our daily lives. Covey makes an essential contribution to our lives by providing a simple and easy 7-Step process to achieve true happiness and contentment.

RICH REFRESH

Part One: YOUR VISION OF THE BEST YOU CAN BE

- Accept that there is ample room for growth in your life.

- Your perceptions are your view of life and form your reality.

- Changing your perceptions changes your life.

- Your paradigm shift is to a "character ethic."

- There are two parts to effectiveness. Who you are and how you interact with others.

Part Two: BECOME THE PERSON YOU WANT TO BE

- This is your self-development that must come before you can effectively work with other people.

Chapter 1: Assuming Leadership of Your Own Life

- There are two important keys to having the life you want – being the leader of your life and managing your life.

- Being proactive wins out over being reactive every time.

- Understanding your circle of influence and how to use it is a key step towards becoming highly effective.

Chapter 2: **Determining the Life You Choose to Lead**

- You begin changing your life by defining the end that you have in mind. This is taking the leadership role in your life.

- Management is taking the proactive steps to make the needed changes.

- Your mission statement is the place you begin making change.

Chapter 3: **Transitioning From Visioning to Living a New Life**

- This is the time to become proactive about the changes you need to make.

- Time management is the key by organizing priorities according to urgency and importance.

- Having your priorities right makes decision making easier.

- The first three habits enable you to live a life based on independent will.

Part Three: PLAYING AND WORKING WELL WITH OTHERS

- Once you are living an effective life based on independent will, you are ready to broaden your effectiveness into all aspects of your life.

- These are trust-based relationships.

Chapter 4: **Win-Win Without Compromise**

- Life does not need to be about winners and losers. An abundant life is about everyone being a winner.

- Winning in life means making decisions that support your principles and values.

- Win-win solutions bring improved relationships today, tomorrow, and continue into the future.

Chapter 5: **Effective Communication**

- Life is all about how we communicate with others.

- Our education teaches us to communicate to others but not to understand what others are communicating to us.

- Listening to understand others is the key to effective communication. Covey calls this "empathic listening."

- Your communication to others must be in a way that makes sense to them as individuals.

Chapter 6: **The Merging of Synergy**

- Synergy brings all of the habits together as the powerful force that makes the biggest changes in your life and the lives of others.

- Synergy brings a new level of creativity beyond what any individual can achieve alone.

- Two effective goals of synergy are exceeding your own limitations and overcoming negative powers that dominate many relationships.

- Synergy works both for individual relationships as well as in organizations.

Part Four: COMPLETING THE CIRCLE AGAIN AND AGAIN

- Habit 7 is not an additional step. You now have the tools that you need.

- As you continue maturing, you only need to continue applying the tools that you now have. This is continuous improvement.

Chapter 7: **Self-Synergy**

- You continue on your path to a fulfilling life by continuing to practice the six habits. This is about constant renewal and improvement. Your personal synergy is the result.

- Renewal includes regular physical exercise, growing spirituality, expanding mentally, and enhancing the social/emotional aspects of your life.

- Once you master the habits on a personal level, you are able to apply these in business and other organizations.

Fun Quiz

Chapter 1: **Assuming Leadership of Your Own Life**

Q. What is Covey's general definition of maturity?

> A. Independent will.

> B. Expressing authority.

> C. Being highly educated.

> D. Having a job.

Chapter 2: **Determining the Life You Choose to Lead**

Q. Which is a key component to taking more control of your life?

> A. Being proactive about everything you do.

> B. Buying your own house.

> C. Never listening to others.

> D. Starting your own business.

Chapter 3: **Transitioning From Visioning to Living a New Life**

Q. Time is a valuable life resource. Which category of time do many people need to pay more attention to?

A. Urgent and important.

B. <u>Not urgent but important.</u>

C. Urgent but not important.

D. Not urgent and not important.

Chapter 4: **Win-Win Without Compromise**

Q. Which is a good definition of a win-win solution?

A. To the victor go the spoils.

B. All participants give up something they want.

C. <u>Both or all participants obtain the goals they want.</u>

D. You give up something this time to gain something next time.

Chapter 5: **Effective Communication**

Q. What element are most people missing when it comes to effective communication?

A. <u>Understanding others begins with empathic listening.</u>

B. Paraphrasing what others say is how you show your full understanding.

C. We have a natural ability to understand others, which means following your gut hunch is the best approach.

D. While listening to others, you need to be thinking about what you will say back to them.

Chapter 6: **The Merging of Synergy**

Q. Why is synergy important in your life?

A. Synergy helps you get the most work out of others.

B. Synergy is your ability to express your authority.

C. Everyone occasionally has a good idea that you should accept.

<u>D. Synergy enables a new level of creativity that is greater than any individual's creativity alone.</u>

Chapter 7: **Self-Synergy**

Q. Habit 7 is about continuous improvement. Which best summarizes how this is accomplished?

A. Reading a new self-help book at least once a year.

B. Asking for a promotion during each work performance review.

C. Regular physical exercise, growing spirituality, expanding mentally, and enhancing the social/emotional aspects of your life.

D. Keeping a journal of your achievements.

Last but not least, remember to visit us at www.summareads.com because we have some really special bonus for you!

This is SummaReads Media, your **#1 learning partner**, signing off right now and we look forward to speaking to you again in another one of our books! Bye for now!

Made in the USA
Middletown, DE
20 February 2021